Love, Fear, Redemption

Reece Banks

Copyright © 2021 Reece Banks

ISBN: 9798513986102

All rights reserved, including the right to reproduce this book, or portions thereof in any form. No part of this text may be reproduced, transmitted, downloaded, decompiled, reverse engineered, or stored, in any form or introduced into any information storage and retrieval system, in any form or by any means, whether electronic or mechanical without the express written permission of the author.

Dear Paige

Thank you for your support.
I hope you enjoy the read!

Love,

Reece
- x -

To my little sister, Jennifer-Rose.

I dedicate this book to you - a rare empathic soul and my anchor in any storm x

Introduction

'**Love, Fear, Redemption**', an emotional outlet allowing me to navigate and understand my thoughts. These three, in my opinion, are the strongest emotions one can feel.

There are subcategories within these three driving emotions, allowing room for exploration. Love is the strongest emotion. Romanticised love, self-love, love of family, love for friends, toxic love, and love for nature are all showcased. This is similarly portrayed with Fear, where the different varieties are all shown in a light that I consider to be honest, authentic and raw. The fear of pain, a loss of identity, overwhelming heartbreak, and sorrow. Finally, I intertwine Redemption, which I believe will be viewed as a curious choice. Redemption differentiates from Revenge as there is a distinctive removal of negative connotations, or as I'm beginning to learn, 'vibrations.' It is forgiving yourself for the past, any mistakes or feelings that have latched, and starting fresh. It is working on yourself, for yourself.

I've already succeeded, and feel incredibly proud to present a book that I feel is an accurate representation of not just my highest work from a literature standpoint, but also an accurate representation of my standpoint as a human. This heightened year has intensified emotions to a vast degree, and to be able to share them in an artistic, creative format is a privilege I feel honoured to have.

What began as a coping mechanism to keep my head above water, soon flourished into something far greater than I could've ever imagined. This being a higher level of confidence in not only who I am as a person, but also in who I am going to become. Publishing this collection was fuelled by a driving motive to instil that same level of clarity in others; to inspire, and to elevate.

- Reece Banks -

- Contents -

Believe	Cry
My Friend	A Memory
Yesterday	JUST A Memory
Skin	Real
Questions	Beautifully Ironic
Perspective	Take Action
Self-Talk	Lesson 101
Storyteller	Vision
The Hero	I'm With You
You & I	Attitude
Seasons	Stardust
Ocean	My Time
Shinrin-Yoku	Encore
Connections	

- Believe -

Speak it into existence.

That dream you have, hold it
in your hands
Describe it, notice how it
expands

What colour is it? How does it
make you feel?
Rejoice as each word creates something
real

Believe it, believe that it is
true. Surge in the strength,
in the power, this is the
breakthrough

Do it for you, for you
alone
It's been if only a minute, look how much
you've grown

- My Friend -

Your footprints mimic those
of mine
mentally, physically, spiritually
our souls intertwine

A hand on my shoulder, you catch me
when I slip
you're with me through thick and thin,
as we survive near-death kayaking trips

No such thing as a life that's
better than yours
we quote J.Cole, for music provides
us with its cure

My friend, I stay grateful
an unconditional, eternal bond
you've got me, I've got you
through this life, and into the beyond

- Yesterday -

It's been years now
Seems like just yesterday to me
So much has happened
So much has changed
Yet, I still stand strong with this belief

The belief that I'm meant to find you
In truth, I know not when
Today
Tomorrow
For less, for more
To find love, or greet a friend

Romance has wondered;
He's found now in the pages of a book
Fantasy or Reality
Who's to say
It depends on where you choose to look

Consistent Inconsistencies
Life is now a guessing game
so much has happened
so much has changed
Yet I still remember
like it was just yesterday

- Skin -

To dream of you while
I'm wide awake
You should come through tonight
a beautiful mistake

Your fingers waltz across
my skin
Overwhelming desire, an
alluring sin

Hard and chiselled, every muscle
defined
She was lithe and shapely,
as if by design

I look up at the stars
in the sky
with the right girl, at the
wrong time

- Questions -

It seems so old-fashioned
the way I find myself thinking
Is this the right era?
The right time?
A place where I'm meant to fit in?

Everything feels off-balance
uncalibrated, a bit skew
The path of simplicity I remember,
did it survive? Was it ever true?

For all we know, we're lost
destined upon this path
But everyone has a purpose, right?
"You've just got to find it first!"

Screw this, what a sadistic game
Innocence has been wounded
And yet you're telling me it's essential to welcome
the pain?

I'm taking my own path.

But I know you'll be there
liaising with Doubt
After all, it's inevitable
you're just choosing when to pounce

- Perspective -

You're told to listen to your elders, they possess a
wisdom you have not yet reached
Yet, have you listened to those younger, those no
taller than your hip or your knee?

They hold happiness, in its purest,
most innocent form
A younger sister guides me far better than
that of the 'norm'

She reminds me to smile, to breathe and
embrace each day
A heavy heart is all-consuming, and still she takes
my hand to go outside and play

Intelligence is relative, there are an abundance of
variants and forms
Emotional intelligence is what I hold most dearly,
she understands and shows me warmth

You're a blessing which I've been gifted
A blessing which I won't forget
A blessing who I love dearly
You're a blessing right on my doorstep

- Self-Talk -

Out of depression and regression, comes progression and a lesson.

- Storyteller -

I want to tell you a story and
this is where it begins
Today
Now
as it does each day, all over again

It's preached to not live in the past,
you're here, so leave it behind
But those were your choices
they were your decisions
and that was your mind

So own it, for it's yours to embrace
Imprinted,
like the ancestors in your palms.
Earned,
like the scars upon your face.

She's calling for you,
Redemption is waiting within
Out of the shadows, she'll appear
Lacing up her boots; you'll win

- The Hero -

The Hero

The Warrior
The Slayer
The Soldier
The Crusader
The Winner
The Healer
The Rescuer
The Leader
The Planner
The Thinker
The Teacher
The Believer
The Writer
The Dreamer

The Hero

- You & I -

When I look at you I see poetry
When I look at you I see the stars
I look at you and feel the power of our
intimate spark

When I look at you I feel whole
When I look at you I feel blessed
I look at you and hear the ocean
kiss the seabed

When I look at you I laugh
When I look at you I cry
I look at you and taste the sweet
opportunity that passed us by

When I look at you I smile
When I look at you I wish
I look at you and reminisce

- Seasons -

You return like Autumn, and
I fall every time

With every step, you're Spring,
reassurance that I'll be fine

Winter is your comfort,
my pillow, my duvet

You shine as bright as Summer, where
night is overcome by day.

- Ocean -

As endless as the ocean,
as timeless as the tides
You don't need big moments to find happiness;
just open your eyes

I sit by the sea, for hours on end
His wisdom guides me, a true, reliable friend
I often fire questions, for which I yearn to learn
His replies are melodic, guiding me through each turn

"You can't stop the waves, but you can learn to surf.
We can't direct the wind, but we can adjust the sails.
Strive for what you believe and
achieve what you deserve
Embrace the chance to change, success is for those
who've learnt to fail."

My gratitude is endless, for the sand in my hair and
the pastel-coloured sky
My seaside town will hold a place in my heart,
forever and always, throughout life's ride

- Shinrin-Yoku -

Step into the forest, stand amongst
the trees
Listen to their thoughts, accept their
offer to breathe

They're here to
guide you
As they've stood the
test of time

Welcome their
embrace
Notice how you feel;
it's a sign

A sign that you're
disconnected
Discombobulated by societies'
noise

A Japanese ancient
practice
An underappreciated
cure to employ

I urge you to plant
yourself
Reconnect with Mother
Earth

It's an absolute
game-changer
Remembrance, renewal,
rebuilding, rebirth

- Connections -

Years from now, much like the years before
a connection can stay strong and so
effortlessly endure

For this is something real,
something worth your time
something beautifully complex, like
conveying understanding through rhyme

Though, understand it you need not do
this is not something you plan, like your next big
career move

Instead, be present
taste the air and feel the sounds
it's like magic; that feeling when your soul
has been found

I'll be right there with you,
to help even out the score
yesterday, today, years from now,
much like the years before

- Cry -

Cry. Please just let me cry.

I clench my fists, squeeze my eyes
Desperate to release the feelings inside

An all-consuming, ever-present thought
Life shifts and you're thrown deep off course

The trees are grey, the sky is brown
I scream and stumble on the uneven ground

One solitary tear falls, temporarily subsiding the pain
I survive, enough to live another day

- A Memory -

Can you remember who
you were,
before the world told you who you
should be?

Can you remember who
you were,
after all these hours you've spent down
on your knees

Can you remember who
you were,
before all the pain, all the fear
all the hurt

Can you remember who
you were,
after all this time – is this not
what you deserve?

- JUST A Memory -

It's okay.

You just forgot who you are.

Welcome back.

- Real -

I'm not okay, but I'm a work in progress
Fed up with hiding these feelings that I
continue to supress

See me for who I am, for each and every day
Not just a highlighted reel off
my insta page

It's ironic, to spread the message of contentment
when I'm not there myself
Take me off the pedestal, remove me from the
highest shelf

I'll try to stay 'authentic', and admit to the
wrongdoings I've made
You'll have my efforts, even through those times
I am afraid

- Beautifully Ironic -

Fear is not real.

Our thoughts have accumulated many years of
experiences, emotions and outcomes.

Depicting a picture; to prevent, protect and prevail.

Beautifully ironic, as our dreams shrivel and
soon turn stale.

It is a product of our imagination, causing us to fear
things that do not at present, and may not ever, exist.

That is borderline insanity, when you
begin to break it down, brick by brick.

Danger is very real, do not read
to misunderstand.

But fear is a choice
be liberated, and take a stand.

- Take Action -

There will always be a distraction to accompany each action

A reason for procrastination if it arises in conversation

Your reply will provide protection, winning over your ego's affection

Hard-work is an infection, your muscles scream in objection

Insecurity feeds on imperfection. This is now your resurrection

Abandon the elusive misdirection. It soon becomes an easy detection

Life takes pride in natural selection. Earn your place through this inspection

Hence forth, a new predilection, you will smile in retrospection

- Lesson 101 -

If you're looking to fly, you must first cut the ties

- Vision -

Is there no better way to live, than to face up
with your head held high
Stone cold, yet with a passion that
burns so bright

What lies before you is a
baptism under fire
Take it in your stride, with all
your belief, all that desire

Right now it's on you, as you face
the one in the mirror
It's in these moments, that
the vision only becomes clearer

Stay relentless, back yourself in
all you seek to achieve
It's one day or day one
Take a breath and believe

- I'm With You -

I'm always going to be there
for you,
even through the times that
I am falling apart

My intuition, my instinct
my heart and soul
they know deeply that you
are my path

You've been there, like
the sun in the day and
the moon in the night

So keep going, Mum
for I'll always hold you close
and have you by my side

- Attitude -

Compare yourself to who you were yesterday, not to who someone else is today

- Stardust -

I'm not worthy

So don't try convince me that

I've got this in the bag

Because ultimately,

I have far too many flaws

And I'm not going to kid myself by saying

There's a real chance for me

(Now read it again, from bottom to top)

- My Time -

This is the start of the new era
mediocre, to meteoric
My rise will be revolutionary
unknown, to historic

- Encore -

It's been more than a
pleasure
to share the thoughts that cross
my mind

I shall feel forever
grateful
to think all it took was for me to
decide

If you're struggling,
reach out
We can be there to help
you through

Envision excitement,
chase dreams
The world is yours
to pursue

Acknowledgements

I have been blessed with many people who have made a difference in my life, and have lent me their hand with this poetry collection. I hold you all in a high regard, and I'll start by thanking those at PublishNation.

I thank you for your assistance, for your advice and for your input. With special thanks to David, who demonstrated patience which is worthy of a knighthood.

To Scott Gaunt, an exceptionally talented designer who created the cover that you hold in your hands. Your skillset is incredible, you harnessed my ideas as my imagination continued to expand.

To my family and friends, what a privilege it is to have a support network as strong as mine. You have my eternal gratitude, which will last the test of time.

To Alasdair McCombe, a man with a unique, quirky, and eccentric teaching style. You instilled a passion for literature within me, which will forever make me smile.

To my parents, for the guidance you've given me this year, the years before and the years to come. You're the best a son could ask for, and I'd like to start here with my Mum.

You're my voice of reason and the first to keep me in check, it is an attribute of yours I cherish and continually respect. At times it is hard to hear, and conflicts with my pride. But you've taught me something which is invaluable, "in a world where you can be anything, be kind."

To Dad, for being my rock, and for showing me the core values of what it takes to be a man. For all those ridiculous memories and moments, which can only stem from that of a work van.

To Jennifer-Rose (and her seal, Snow), for showing me what love means. You're the first to ask me if I'm okay, and show me that not all is as it seems. Your innocence is beautiful, and provides me with the perspective I need. With you both, a laugh is simply guaranteed.

Lastly, I'd like to leave this as a final note. I will donate 10% of every book sale to 'The Samaritans', a charity who helped me when I thought I'd lost all hope.

Samaritans Free Helpline: 116 123

For more poetry, visit my Instagram page:

@reecebankswrites

Printed in Great Britain
by Amazon